ᒥᑦᑎᒪᑕᓕᓐᒧᐊᕐᓂᕋ
My Trip to Pond Inlet

ᑎᑎᕋᖅᑐᖅ
ᓵᓚᒨᓂ ᐊᕙ
ᑎᑎᖅᑐᒐᖅᑐᖅ
ᐃᒪ ᐲᑐᓯᓐ

WRITTEN BY
Solomon Awa
ILLUSTRATED BY
Emma Pedersen

ᓵᓗᒨᓂ ᐊᕿᐅᔪᖕᒐ. ᖃᐅᖕᓇᕐᒥ ᐱᕈᖅᓴᓚᐅᖅᑐᖕᒐ ᓄᓇᕗᒻᒥ.

ᐅᓂᒃᑳᕐᓂᐊᕋᒪ ᐊᐅᓪᓚᓇᐊᖅᑲᓚᐅᖅᓯᒪᓂᓐᓂ ᒥᑦᑎᒪᑕᓕᖕᒧᑦ ᓄᓇᑦᑕ ᐊᓯᐊᓄᑦ. ᐅᓪᓗᓕᒫᖅ ᖃᐅᖕᓇᕐᒥ ᐃᖕᒋᕐᕋᓇᖅᑐᖅ ᐅᒥᐊᒃᑯᑦ. ᐃᖅᑲᐅᒪᐅᔭᐃᓐᓇᕐᓂᐊᕋᒃᑯ ᒥᑦᑎᒪᑕᓕᖕᒧᐊᕐᓂᓇᓚᐅᖅᓯᒪᔭᕋ.

My name is Solomon.
I grew up in a place called Qaungnaq in Nunavut.

I am going to tell you a story about a time when I had to travel to a community called Pond Inlet. It is a day's journey from Qaungnaq by boat. I will always remember my time in Pond Inlet.

ᓱᕈᓯᐅᑎᓪᓗᖓ ᖃᐅᓐᓇᕐᒥ, ᐊᐅᔭᒃᑯᑦ ᓄᓇᒋᓚᐅᖅᓯᒪᒐᑦᑎᒍᑦ. ᑐᐱᕐᒥᐅᑕᐅᓚᐅᖅᓯᒪᔪᒍᑦ ᖃᑯᖅᑕᑯᒃᓱᐊᓗᖕᒥᒃ. ᑐᐱᖅ ᑐᐱᒃᓴᔭᓪᓚᑦᑖᖑᓪᓗᓂ ᐃᔾᔪᓪᓗᓂ ᐊᖏᔫᒻᒪᑦ ᓈᒻᒪᓚᐅᖅᓯᒪᔪᖅ ᐅᕙᓐᓄᑦ, ᐊᓈᓇᓐᓄᑦ, ᐊᑖᑕᓐᓄᑦ, ᖃᑕᖕᖑᑎᓕᒫᕌᓗᑦᑎᓐᓄᓪᓗ. ᐃᓚᔮᕈᑦᑕᐅᖅ ᐊᓯᒋᑦ ᓄᓇᖅᑲᑎᒋᓚᐅᖅᓯᒪᔭᕋᑦ. ᓂᖓᐅᑦᑕ ᐊᖓᔪᖅᑳᖕᒥᒃ ᐃᓪᓗᕋᖓᕐᒥᐅᑕᐅᓚᐅᖅᓯᒪᔪᑦ.

ᐅᓂᒃᑳᖅ ᑖᓐᓇ ᐱᒋᐊᕐᓂᐊᖅᑐᖅ ᐊᐅᔭᖖᑯᕋᑖᖅᓯᒪᑎᓪᓗᒍ. ᓯᑯᐃᖅᓯᒪᓕᖅᑎᓪᓗᒍ ᐅᖅᓱᐊᑦᑎᐊᖅᑐᓂᓗ. ᐊᖑᓇᓱᒃᑲᑦᑎᐊᕚᓪᓗᓂ.

When I was a child in Qaungnaq, we lived in a camp in the summer. We slept in a big, thick tent. The tent was so big that it fit me, my mother, my father, and all my siblings. Other families had tents there too, and my brother-in-law's parents had a cabin.

This story starts in the early summer. The ice had drifted and the water was calm. It was the perfect season for hunting.

ᒥᓂᒐᓛᒃᑎᑦᑐᒍ, ᐅᒥᐊᒃᑯᑦ ᐊᖑᑎᓕᒫᑦᑎᐊᑦ ᐊᐅᓪᓚᖅᓯᒪᑎᑦᑐᒋᑦ. ᑐᐱᕐᒦᑦᑐᐃᓐᓇᑦᑎᐊᖑᑎᑦᑐᑕᓕ ᒪᓴᒧᒪᖖᒋᓐᓇᑦᑕ.

ᐊᓈᓇᒐ ᓇᓄᕕᓂᕐᒥᒃ ᖁᓪᓕᕐᒥᓄᑦ ᖁᓕᑦᓯᖅᑎᑦᑐᒍ ᐅᒃᑯᓯᖕᒧᑦ ᓂᕕᖕᒐᔪᒧᑦ ᐆᑦᑎᔭᖓ. ᐅᓪᓛᒃᑯᑦ ᖁᓕᑦᓯᓕᖅᑲᒻᒥᖖᒋᑕᖓ. ᐅᖅᑲᖅᐸᓚᐅᖅᓯᒪᖕᒪᑦ ᓇᓄᕕᓃᒡᒎᖅ ᐊᑯᓂ ᐆᑦᑎᔭᓇᐊᖅᑲᖅᒪᑕ.

One rainy day, all the men were out hunting by boat. My mother and sister and I stayed in our tent because we didn't want to get wet.

My mother was cooking polar bear meat in a big pot of water that hung above the *qulliq.** She had started cooking it early in the morning. She always said you need to cook polar bear meat for a very long time to prepare it well.

***qulliq** (KOO-leek): seal oil lamp

ᐅᒃᑯᓯᒃ ᐆᓇᖅᓯᔪᐊᓘᑦᑐᓂ ᖃᔮᖕᒐᓗ ᖃᖄᖅᑐᓂ. ᐊᓅᓇᒪ
ᐅᒃᑯᓯᖕᒨᖅᑕᐃᓕᕐᑯᑦᑐᓂᑎᒍᑦ ᐆᕐᓴᕐᓂᐊᕋᑦᑕ.

ᒥᓂᑦᑐᒍ ᒪᓴᒍᒪᖖᒋᓐᓇᑦᑕ ᐃᓯᖅᓯᒪᑐᐃᓐᓇᖅᓗᑕ, ᓇᔭᑯᓗᓚᓗ
ᖁᕕᐊᕆᓛᑦᑎᓐᓂᒃ ᐱᖖᒍᐊᓕᖅᑐᓄᒃ. ᓯᕗᓪᓕᕐᒥ ᐸᐃᑉᐹᑯᓗᖕᒥᒃ ᐅᕐᑯᒻᒥᖅᓯᕙᒃᑐᓄᒃ
ᖃᐅᓯᓕᖅᑎᑉᐸᒃᓗᑎᒍ. ᑭᒍᑎᑦᑎᓐᓄᑦ ᐊᖕᒪᓗᖅᓯᑎᑉᐸᒃᓗᑎᒍᒃ. ᑎᓯᒃᑎᑦᑕᕌᖕᒐᑦ,
ᒥᓗᕆᐊᕈᑎᒋᕙᒃᓗᑎᒍᒃ.

The pot grew hot and the water boiled. My mother told us to stay away from the pot because it was so hot it could burn us.

Since we were stuck inside while it rained, my sister and I started to play our favourite game. First we put a bit of paper in our mouths to wet it. Then we rolled the paper into balls using our teeth. When the balls hardened, we threw them at each other.

ᓇᔭᒐᓗ ᐅᓪᓚᔭᒃᓱᓄᒃ ᐊᒡᕖᖅᑲᑦᑕᐅᑎᓇᓱᐊᖅᐸᒃᓱᓄᒃ, ᒥᓗᖅᑕᐅᑦᑕᐃᓕᒪᓪᓗᓄᒃ. ᐊᓈᓇᒪ ᑐᓄᐊᓄᑦ ᐃᔨᕆᐊᓚᐅᖅᓱᖓ ᐃᒡᓕᖅᒥ ᐃᒃᓯᕚᖅᑎᓪᓗᒍ ᐳᐊᓗᓕᐅᖅᑎᓪᓗᒍ ᐃᖅᑲᖅᑏᖕᓂᒃ.

ᐃᒡᓕᓯᖅ ᑐᑎᒥᐊᖅᓱᒍ, ᖁᕕᐊᓯᐊᓗᐊᒧᑦ ᑕᐅᓄᖓ ᓇᑎᖁᑦ ᑐᑎᒐᒪ ᐅᒃᐱᑲᖅᓱᖓ ᖁᓪᓕᐅᑉ ᓴᓂᐊᓄᑦ. ᑖᓐᓇ ᑕᓕᖓ ᓴᐅᒥᒐ ᐅᒃᑯᓯᖕᒧᑦ ᖁᓚᑦᓯᖅᑐᒧᑦ ᑲᐅᔪᐊᓘᓪᓗᓂ!

My sister and I dodged all over the place, trying not to get hit by paper balls. I ducked behind my mother where she sat on the bed, sewing a pair of waterproof mittens.

But when I stepped off the edge of the bed, I was too excited by the game. I didn't pay attention and I tripped. I fell toward the qulliq and the cooking pot. My left arm landed right in the boiling hot water!

ᑕᓕᕋ ᐅᒃᑯᓯᖕᒥ ᐋᕋᒃᑯ ᕿᐊᓯᑲᐅᑎᒋᓪᓗᖕᒐ ᐃᕋᕐᓗᖕᒐ. ᖃᖄᕐᒧᑦ ᑕᓕᕋ ᐆᕐᑐᐊᓘᓪᓗᓂ.

ᐊᓈᓇᒪ ᑕᓕᕋ ᖃᐅᔾᔨᒋᐊᖅᑲᓗᓂᐅᒃ. ᐅᕕᓂᖕᒐ ᐊᐅᐸᖅᓯᓪᓗᓂ ᐋᓐᓂᐊᖅᑐᐊᓘᓪᓗᓂ. ᐊᓈᓇᒪ ᐊᓪᓚᕆᐊᕋᓗᐊᕐᒪᒍ ᐅᕕᓂᒐ ᖃᐅᑐᐃᓐᓇᖅᑲᓗᓂ, ᐊᐅᓕᖅᑲᓗᓂᓗ! ᐊᓈᓇᒪ ᓴᐃᒪᑎᓐᓇᔪᒃᑲᓗᓂᖕᒐ.

I yanked my arm out of the pot and started wailing in pain. The boiling water had burned me badly.

My mother quickly came to me to check my arm. My skin turned bright red and it hurt. She tried to wipe away the hot water, but the skin came right off where she touched me, and I started to bleed! My mother comforted me as I cried in pain.

ᐊᓈᓇᒪ ᐃᒻᒧᓯᖅᓱᓂᐅᒃ ᖃᓪᓗᓈᖅᑕᒥᒃ. ᖁᑲᕋᓱᒃᑲᓗᐊᖅᑐᖓ, ᑭᓯᐊᓂ ᑕᓕᕋ ᐋᓐᓂᐊᓗᐊᖅᓱᓂ. ᓇᔭᒐ ᐃᑲᔪᖅᓱᓂ ᐃᓐᓇᖅᓱᖓ ᐋᓐᓂᐊᕈᓐᓃᖅᓯᖅᓱᖓ.

ᐅᐊᑦᑎᐊᕈᓐᖑᖅᑎᓪᓗᒍ, ᐊᑖᑕᒃᑯᒃᑲ ᐊᖑᓇᓱᑦᑎᐊᖅᓯᒪᔪᓪᓗ ᑎᑭᑦᑐᑎᒃ. ᓂᐅᕝᕕᐅᓚᐊᕈᓐᓇᙱᑦᑐᖓᓘᓐᓃᑦ ᐋᓐᓂᐊᖅᑐᐊᓘᒐᒪ.

My mother wrapped my burned arm in a cloth. I tried to sit still, but my arm hurt so much. Then my sister helped me to my bed so I could get some rest.

Later that day, my father and the rest of the hunters returned to the camp. I was in too much pain to go and greet them.

ᐊᓈᓇᒪ ᐊᑖᑕᒐ ᐅᖃᐅᑎᓪᓗᓂᐅᒃ ᖃᓄᐃᓕᖕᒪᖕᖔᕐᒪ. ᒪᑦᑐᓯᖅᓯᒪᓂᕋ ᒪᑉᐱᕋᒥᐅᒃ ᑕᓕᕋ ᑕᑯᓪᓗᓂᐅᒃ. "ᐅᓇᔫᖅ ᐆᔾᔪᐊᖅᓯᒪᔪᖅ ᐋᓐᓂᐊᕕᓕᐊᕆᐊᖃᖅᑐᑦ ᒥᕐᑎᒪᑕᓕᖕᒧᑦ."

ᐊᐅᓪᓚᑲᐅᑎᒋᓪᓗᑕ ᒥᕐᑎᒪᑕᓕᖕᒧᑦ ᐅᒥᐊᒃᑯᑦ. ᐅᓐᓄᐊᒃᑯᑦ, ᐅᖅᓯᐊᕐᑎᐊᖅᓱᓂᓗ. ᐊᐅᓚᓇᕋᓂ. ᓯᓂᓕᕐᓕᖅᓱᖓ ᐃᖏᕐᕋᓪᓗᑕ.

My mother told my father what had happened. He peeled the cloth back and looked at my arm. He said, “This is a serious burn. We need to take you to the health centre in Pond Inlet.”

We set off right away by boat to Pond Inlet. It was the middle of the night, and the water was calm and still. I fell asleep while we were travelling.

ᓯᓂᓪᓚᕆᒃᑐᐊᓘᓕᕐᓂᕋᒪ ᖃᐅᔨᓐᓂᙱᒻᒪᕆᒃᑐᖓ ᑎᑭᓐᓂᕋᓗᐊᕋᑦᑕ. ᐊᖓᔪᒪ ᑐᐹᕆᐊᖃᓚᐅᕌᖓ. ᐅᓪᓛᖑᓕᖅᓱᑕ ᒥᑦᑎᒪᑕᓕᖕᒦᓕᖅᓱᑕ.

ᐋᓐᓂᐊᕕᓕᐊᑲᐅᑎᒋᓪᓗᑕ. ᐋᓐᓂᐊᓯᐅᖅᑎᐅᑉ ᑲᒪᒋᑦᑎᐊᖅᑐᓂᖓ. ᖃᓪᓗᓈᖅᑕ ᐊᓈᓇᒪ ᐃᒻᒧᓯᐅᑎᒋᓚᐅᖅᑕᖓ ᐲᖅᑐᓂᐅᒃ. ᑕᓕᕋ ᐋᓐᓂᐊᖅᑐᐊᓘᓪᓗᓂ, ᑭᓯᐊᓂ ᓂᑲᒋᓪᓗᖓ.

ᐋᓐᓂᐊᒐᓗᐊᖅᑐᖓ ᐊᓂᖅᓵᖅᑐᑦᑎᐊᕋᓱᐃᓐᓇᖅᓱᖓ.

I slept so deeply that I didn't even notice when we arrived. My brother had to wake me up. It was morning and we were in Pond Inlet.

We went straight to the health centre. A nurse took care of me. She removed the cloth my mother had wrapped around my wound. My arm hurt a lot, but she was very gentle.

I tried to be strong and breathe through the pain.

ᐋᓐᓂᐊᓯᐅᖅᑎᐅᑉ ᐊᐱᕆᓪᓗᓂᖓ ᖃᓄᖅ ᐆᓐᓂᕐᒪᖔᕐᒪ ᐅᖃᐅᑎᓪᓗᒍ ᓇᔾᑲᓗ ᐱᙳᐊᓚᐅᕋᓐᓄᒃ ᖁᕙᐊᑦᑕᓗᐊᒧᑦ ᐅᕿᓚᐅᕐᓂᖃᖅᑐᖓ ᑎᖅᑎᑦᑐᒧᑦ ᖁᓕᑦᓯᖅᑐᒧᑦ ᓇᓄᕕᓂᕐᒧᑦ.

ᐃᖅᑲᐃᑎᕐᕆᓂᖓ ᐅᔾᔨᖅᓱᑎᐊᖅᑲᑦᑕᖅᑯᓪᓗᓂᖓ ᑎᖅᑎᑦᑑᑉ ᖃᓂᒋᔮᓂ.

The nurse asked me how I burned my arm. I told her about the game my sister and I had been playing and how I got too excited and fell into the boiling pot of polar bear meat.

She reminded me to always be careful around boiling water.

ᐋᓐᓂᐊᓯᐅᖅᑎᐅᑉ ᑕᓕᕋ ᒪᑦᑐᓯᖅᓱᓈᕐᒪᒍ,
ᐃᓐᓇᖅᑎᑦᑐᓂᖓ ᐋᓐᓂᐊᕕᒻᒥ ᓯᓂᖕᓂᐊᕋᒪ.

ᐊᓈᓇᒪ ᐊᓈᓇᒃᑯᖕᒋᑦ ᒥᑦᑎᒪᓕᖕᒥᐅᑕᐅᖕᒪᑎᒃ, ᐊᑖᑕᒐ
ᐊᖕᒐᔪᒐᓗ ᑕᐃᑯᖕᒐ ᓯᓂᒋᐊᖅᑐᕐᓂᖅᓲᑎᒃ.

When the nurse finished bandaging my arm, she took me to a bed in the health centre so I could sleep.

My mother's parents lived in Pond Inlet, so my father and brother went there for the night.

ᐅᓪᓛᒃᑯᑦ ᐃᖅᑯᒻᒪᕋᒪ, ᐊᑖᑕᒐ
ᐊᖓᔪᒐᓗ ᐋᓐᓂᐊᕕᒻᒦᓐᓇᑎᒃ. ᑕᓕᕋᓗ
ᐊᑲᐅᓂᖅᓴᐅᓕᖅᑐᓂ. ᒪᕐᑐᓯᖅᓱᖅᓯᒪᒐᒪ,
ᐋᓐᓂᐊᓯᐅᖅᑎᐅᑉ ᐃᓪᓕᕐᒦᖕᒋᓐᓇᕐᑯᓪᓗᓂᖓ.

ᐅᓪᓘᓕᖅᑎᓪᓗᒍ, ᐊᑖᑕᒐ
ᐊᖓᔪᒐᓗ ᐋᓐᓂᐊᕕᖕᒧᑦ ᐅᑎᖅᑐᑎᒃ.
ᐊᑲᐅᓂᖅᓴᐅᓕᖅᓱᖓᓗ, ᐊᓂᔪᓐᓇᖅᓯᓪᓗᖓ.

ᐋᓐᓂᐊᓯᐅᖅᑎᐅᑉ ᐅᖃᐅᑎᓪᓗᓂᖓ
ᒥᕐᑎᒪᑕᓕᖕᒦᒃᑯᒪᒍᖅ ᓈᒻᒪᖕᓂᖅᓴᐅᓂᐊᖅᑐᖅ.
ᑕᐃᒫᒃ ᑕᓕᕋ ᖃᐅᔾᔮᖕᒍᖃᑦᑕᕐᓂᐊᕐᒪᑦ
ᒪᒥᑉᐸᓪᓕᐊᑎᓪᓗᒍ.

When I woke up the next morning, my father and brother were not there. My arm felt much better. I was bandaged up, and the nurse said I should stay in bed.

Later that day, my father and brother returned to the health centre. I was feeling much better, and I was allowed to go outside.

The nurse told us that it would be best for me to stay in Pond Inlet for a little while. That way they could keep an eye on my arm as it healed.

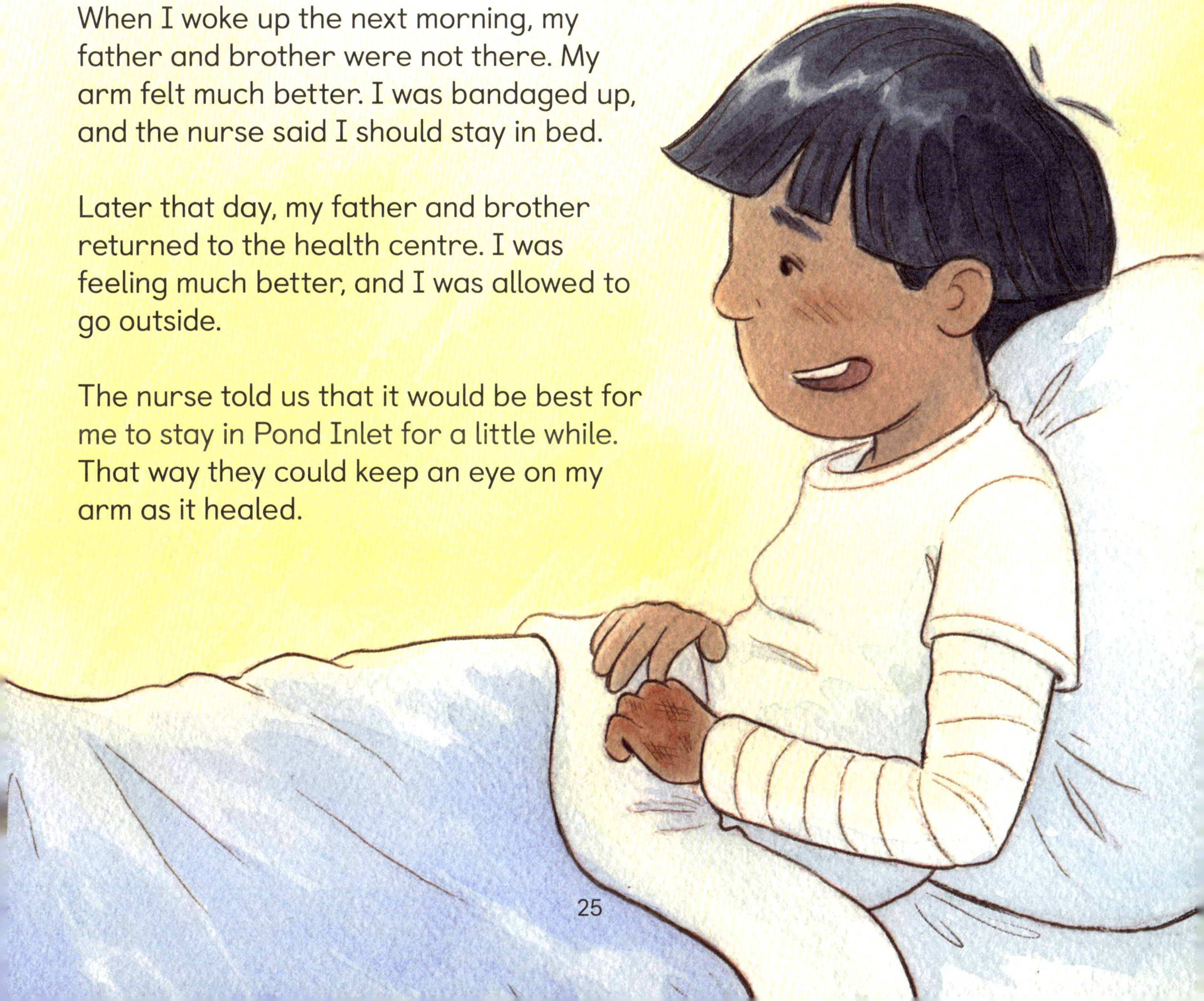

ᓄᓇᓕᖕᓂ ᓄᕗᓕᒃᑕᖅᑲᕐᒪᑦ ᐃᓪᓗᓂᒃ ᐃᓕᓐᓂᐊᖅᑎᓄᑦ ᓇᔪᖅᑕᐅᓲᓂᒃ. ᑕᐃᑲᓃᑲᐃᓐᓇᕐᓂᐊᖅᖢᖓ ᑕᓕᒐ ᒪᒥᑦᑎᕐᓂᖓᓂᒃ.

ᑕᐃᒃᑯᓄᖕᖓ ᐃᒡᓗᓄᑦ ᐱᓱᒃᑐᑕ ᐋᓐᓂᐊᕕᐅᑉ ᖃᓂᒋᔮᓃᒻᒪᑕ.

ᐃᓯᖁᒪ, ᑕᒪᒃᑯᐊᓕ ᓱᐳᔭᐊᓗᐃᑦ ᑕᕝᕙᓃᑦᑐᖅ! ᐋᓪᓚᔪᐊᓚᐅᖁᓗᐊᖅᖢᖓ, ᑐᙵᓵᖅᑕᐅᒐᒪ ᐋᓪᓚᔪᐊᕈᓐᓃᖅᖢᖓ. ᐱᙳᐊᖅᑲᑎᒋᓕᖅᖢᒋᑦ ᐱᖅᑲᓐᓇᕆᓕᖅᖢᒋᑦ.

There was a special house in the community where students stayed. I was going to live there while my arm healed.

We walked over to a pointed house next to the health centre.

When I walked in, there were so many other children! I felt shy at first, but they were all so welcoming. I quickly started playing and making new friends.

ᐊᑖᑕᒐ ᐊᖓᔪᒐᓗ ᑕᒫᓃᑲᐃᓐᓇᓚᐅᖅᑐᑎᒃ. ᖃᐅᖕᓇᕐᒧᑦ ᐅᑎᕆᐊᖅᑲᓯᖅᑐᑎᒃ.

ᖁᕕᐊᓱᑦᑎᐊᖅᑐᖓ ᓱᕈᓯᐅᖃᑎᒃᑲ ᐱᖃᑎᒋᖃᑦᑕᓯᕋᒃᑭᑦ ᑕᓯᕋ ᒪᒥᑦᑎᕐᓂᖓᓂ. ᐱᖃᓐᓇᕆᔭᖅᑖᕆᓪᓗᒍ ᓄᑲᑉᐱᐊᑦ ᐃᓚᖓᑦ. ᖁᕕᐊᓱᒃᑐᓄᒃ ᐱᙳᐊᖃᑎᒌᖃᑦᑕᖅᑐᓄᒃ.

My father and brother stayed for a few days. Then they returned to the camp at Qaungnaq.

I was happy living with the other children while my arm healed. I became good friends with one boy. We had fun playing together.

ᒥᑦᑎᒪᑕᓕᒃ ᑕᐃᔅᓯᒪᓂ ᐊᖏᓂᖅᓵᓘᓚᐅᖅᓯᒪᖕᒪᑦ ᖃᐅᖕᓇᕐᒥ. ᐊᑕᐅᓯᕐᒥᒃ ᐃᓪᓗᕋᓛᖅᑕᖃᖅᖢᓂ ᑐᐹᑦᑐ ᓄᓇᑦᑎᓐᓂ – ᑖᓐᓇᓕ ᐅᐸᒃᑕᕋ ᐃᓪᓗᖃᖅᖢᓂ ᐊᒥᓱᐊᓗᖕᓂᒃ! ᐊᓯᖏᓐᓂᓪᓗ ᐃᓪᓗᑕᖃᐅᖅᖢᓂ, ᐋᓐᓂᐊᕕᒃᑕᖃᖅᖢᓂ ᑐᒃᓯᐊᕐᕕᒃᑕᖃᖅᖢᓂᓗ. ᒪᑦᑐᓯᖅᓱᖅᓯᒪᔪᖅ ᑕᓕᕋ ᓂᑲᒋᒋᐊᖃᓚᐅᖅᓯᒪᔭᕋ, ᐱᖃᓐᓇᕆᔭᒃᑲ ᑭᓯᐊᓂ ᐱᖃᑎᒋᒋᐊᖓ ᖁᕕᐊᓇᓚᐅᖅᓯᒪᔪᖅ. ᕿᓚᒥᐊᓗᒃ ᑕᐅᕙᓃᓚᐅᖅᓯᒪᔪᖓ!

Pond Inlet was so much bigger than Qaungnaq. We had just one cabin and some tents in our camp—this community had so many houses! There were other buildings too, like the health centre and the church. I had to be careful with my arm, but I had fun exploring with my friends. The time went by fast!

ᐱᓇᓱᐊᕈᓯᕐᔫᓐᓃᑦ ᓈᒻᒪᑦ, ᐋᓐᓂᐊᓱᐅᖅᑎᐅᑉ ᐅᖃᐅᑎᓚᐅᖅᓯᒪᒑᖕᒐ ᐊᖕᒋᕐᕋᕈᓐᓇᖅᓯᓂᕋᖅᓱᓂᖕᒐ. ᐅᕝᕙᓂᒐᒎᖅ ᒪᒥᓐᓇᓲᔭᕐᓂᐊᖅᑐᖅ ᐊᑦᑕᕐᓇᕈᓐᓃᕐᒪᒡᒎᖅ.

ᐊᑖᑕᒪ ᐊᖕᒐᔪᒪᓗ ᐊᖕᒋᕐᕋᐅᑎᔭᖅᑐᕆᓇᓪᓗᓂᖕᒐ. ᐅᑦᓗᕆᒫᑦᑎᐊᖅ ᒥᑦᑎᒪᑕᕆᖕᒥ ᖅᑲᐅᓐᓇᕐᔫᖅᓱᓚᐅᖅᑐᒍᑦ ᐅᒥᐊᒃᑯᑦ.

ᖁᕕᐊᒋᓚᐅᖅᓯᒪᔭᖅ ᒥᑦᑎᒪᑕᕆᖕᒦᔅᓱᖕᒐ
ᐱᖃᓐᓇᕆᔭᖅᑖᖅᑐᖃᒪ ᑕᐅᕙᓂ,
ᖁᕕᐊᓲᖅᑐᖕᒐᓗ ᐊᖕᒋᕐᕋᒪ!

After a week or so, the nurse who had been taking care of me said I was ready to go home. It would take time for my skin to heal fully, but I was out of danger.

My dad and brother came to take me home. We travelled the whole day from Pond Inlet to Qaungnaq in a boat.

I enjoyed staying in Pond Inlet and made good friends there, but I was also happy to be home!

ᖃᓄᐃᓕᐅᕈᑏᑦ ᐊᖕᒋᔪᖅᑳᓇᔭᐅᔪᓄᑦ ᐃᓕᓴᐃᔨᓄᓪᓗ

Activities for Parents and Teachers

ᐅᖃᖃᑎᒌᓪᓗᒃ!

ᐊᐱᕆᖅᑕᑦᑕᕈᑎᒃ ᓱᕈᓰᑦ ᐃᓱᒪᔪᓐᓇᖅᓯᕚᓪᓕᐊᓰᖑᒍᑦ ᐊᒃᑐᐊᓂᖅᒥᓂᒃ ᐅᓂᒃᑳᒧᑦ, ᐅᖃᓕᒫᒃᓴᕚᒃᑐᑎᒡᓗ ᐅᖃᓪᓚᒍᓐᓇᖅᓯᑦᑎᐊᖅᐸᒃᑐᑎᒃ ᓈᓚᒍᓐᓇᖅᓯᑦᑎᐊᖅᐸᒃᑐᑎᒡᓗ. ᐅᖃᓕᒫᕈᒃ ᒥᑦᑎᒪᑕᓕᖒᐊᖅᓂᕋ ᐊᑕᐅᓯᐊᕐᓗᒍ. ᑕᐃᒪ ᐅᖃᓕᒫᓕᖅᑭᖕᒥᓗᒍ ᐊᐱᕆᓕᕐᒥᓗᒋᑦ ᐅᑯᐊ ᐊᐱᖅᑯᑏᑦ:

- ᓱᓘᓂᒃᑯᒃ ᓇᔭᒌᒃ ᖃᓄᖅ ᐱᙳᐊᓚᐅᖅᐹᒃ?
- ᓱᓘᓂ ᖃᓄᐃᓕᖓᓂᖅᐸ ᐱᙳᐊᖅᑎᓪᓗᒋᒃ?
- ᓱᓘᓂ ᓇᒧᑦ ᐊᐅᓪᓚᕆᐊᖅᑲᓚᐅᖅᐸ?
- ᖃᓄᖅ ᓱᓘᓂ ᑕᐅᕗᙵᓚᐅᖅᐸ?
- ᖃᓄᖅ ᖃᐅᖕᓇᖅ ᒥᑦᑎᒪᑕᓕᒡᓗ ᐊᔾᔩᙱᒋᓛᒃ? ᓇᓕᐊᒃ ᓄᓇᓕᒃᔪᐊᖑᓂᖅᓴᐅᕙ?

Let’s Talk!

Asking questions encourages young children to think about and connect with the story, as well as to practise using their vocabulary and speaking and listening skills. Read *My Trip to Pond Inlet* once through. Then read the story again and ask the following questions as you read:

- What game did Solomon play with his sister?
- What happened to Solomon while he was playing?
- Where did Solomon travel to?
- How did Solomon get there?
- How are Qaungnaq and Pond Inlet different? Which community is bigger?

ᓇᒧᙱᓚᐅᖅᓯᒪᕕᑦ?

ᐅᕙᓂ ᐱᓕᕆᐊᒃᓴᒥ, ᓱᕈᓰᑦ ᐅᓂᒃᑳᕐᓂᐊᖅᑐᑦ ᐊᑐᓚᐅᖅᓯᒪᔭᒥᓂᒃ ᐃᓱᒪᒋᔭᒥᓂᒡᔪᓐᓃᑦ ᓄᓇᓕᖕᒨᕆᐅᕋᒥᒃ. ᑕᐃᒪ ᑎᑎᖅᑐᒐᓕᕐᓂᐊᕐᒥᔪᑦ ᐊᑐᖅᓯᒪᔭᒥᓂᒃ ᐃᓱᒪᒋᔭᒥᓂᒡᔪᓐᓃᑦ.

ᐊᔪᕆᖅᓯᐅᔾᔨᔾᔭᑎᑦ

1. ᓱᕈᓰᑦ ᐊᐱᕆᒃᑭᑦ ᐃᖅᑲᐅᒪᖕᒪᖕᒑᑕ ᓲᓗᒨᓂ ᓇᒧᙱᓚᕆᐊᖃᓚᐅᕐᒪᖕᒑᑦ ᓱᖕᒪᓪᓗ ᑕᐅᕗᙱᓚᕆᐊᖃᓚᐅᕐᒪᖕᒑᑦ. ᐊᐱᕆᒃᑭᑦ ᐃᖅᑲᐅᒪᖕᒪᖕᒑᑕ ᖃᓄᖅ ᓲᓗᒨᓂ ᐃᒃᐱᒍᓱᓚᐅᕐᒪᖕᒑᑦ ᒥᑦᑎᒪᑕᓕᖕᒦᑎᓪᓗᒍ. ᑎᑎᕋᕈᒪᑐᐃᓐᓇᕆᐊᖃᖅᑕᑎᑦ ᓱᕈᓰᑦ ᑭᒡᒍᑎᖕᒋᑦ.
2. ᓱᕈᓰᑦ ᐊᐱᕆᒃᑭᑦ ᓄᓇᓕᖕᓅᓚᐅᖅᓯᒪᖕᒪᖕᒑᑕ ᐅᐸᓚᐅᖅᓯᒪᙱᑕᒥᓄᑦ. ᓱᕈᓯᓕᒫᑦ ᐃᓚᖕᒋᓪᓘᓐᓃᑦ ᐊᖕᒋᖅ<ᑕ, ᐊᐱᕆᒃᑭᑦ ᖃᓄᖅ ᐅᐸᓚᐅᖅᓯᒪᙱᑕᒥᓃᑦᑐᑎᒃ ᐃᒃᐱᒍᓱᓚᐅᖅᓯᒪᖕᒪᖕᒑᑕ. ᓱᕈᓯᓕᒫᑦ ᐃᓚᖕᒋᓪᓘᓐᓃᑦ ᐋᒃᑳᖅ<ᑕ, ᐅᐸᓚᐅᖅᓯᒪᔪᒪᔭᒥᓂᒃ ᐃᓱᒪᕐᑯᒃᑭᑦ ᖃᓄᕐᓗ ᐃᒃᐱᒍᓱᒃᑲᔭᕐᒪᖕᒑᑕ ᑕᐃᑲᓃᑉ<ᑕ. ᓄᓇᓪᓚᕆᐅᔪᓐᓇᖅᑐᖅ ᓄᓇᙳᐊᕐᓗᓐᓃᑦ.
3. ᓱᕈᓰᑦ ᐃᓱᒪᑎᒃᑲᓐᓂᕋᓱᓪᓗᒋᑦ ᐊᑐᖅᓯᒪᔭᒥᖕᓂᒃ ᐃᓱᒪᒋᔭᒥᓂᒡᔪᓐᓃᑦ, ᐅᑯᓂᖓ ᐊᐱᕆᔪᓐᓇᕐᒥᔭᑎᑦ:
   - ᖃᓄᐃᒻᒪᑦ ᑕᐅᕗᙱᓚᐅᖅᓯᒪᕕᑦ? ᖃᓄᐃᒻᒪᓪᓗᓐᓃᑦ ᑕᐅᕗᙱᓛᕈᒪᕕᑦ? ᓲᕐᓗ, ᐃᓚᖕᒋᑦ ᐊᐅᓪᓚᓲᖑᖕᒪᑕ ᓄᖅᑲᖕᒐᔭᖅᑐᖅᑐᑎᒃ, ᐃᓚᒥᓄᑦ ᓂᐅᕐᕈᓪᓗᑎᒃ, ᐋᓐᓂᐊᕕᓕᐊᖅᑐᑎᒡᓗᓐᓃᑦ.
   - ᖃᓄᖅ ᑕᐅᕗᙱᓚᐅᖅᓯᒪᕕᑦ? ᐅᕝᕙᓗᓐᓃᑦ ᖃᓄᖅ ᑕᐅᕗᙱᖅᑐᖅᑲᓲᖑᖕᒪᑦ?
   - ᖃᓄᖅ ᐃᒃᐱᖕᓇᔪᕙ ᐊᖕᒋᕐᕋᕐᒦᓐᓇᓂ? ᖃᓄᖅ ᐃᒃᐱᖕᓇᕋᔭᖅᑐᕆᕕᐅᒃ?
   - ᖃᓄᖅ ᓄᓇᔅᓯ ᐊᔾᔨ<ᓗᒋᓚᐅᖅ<, ᖃᓄᖅ ᐊᔾᔨᒋᓚᐅᙱᒋᓛ? ᐅᕝᕙᓗᓐᓃᑦ ᖃᓄᖅ ᐊᔾᔨᕐᑲ<ᓗᒃ<ᓪᓚᐃᒐᔭᖅ< ᐊᔾᔨᕐᑲᕋᔭᙱᓚᕐᓗᓐᓃᑦ?
4. ᓱᕈᓯᓕᒫᑦ ᐃᓚᖕᒋᓪᓘᓐᓃᑦ ᐅᐸᓚᐅᖅᓯᒪᙱᑕᒥᓅᖅᓯᒪᒃ<ᑕ, ᐊᔾᔨᙳᐊᒥᒃ ᑎᑎᖅᑐᒐᖅᑎᓪᓗᒋᑦ ᓂᐅᕐᕈᕕᒋᓚᐅᖅᓯᒪᔭᒥᓄᑦ. ᑕᒪᐃᑕ ᐃᓚᖕᒋᓪᓘᓐᓃᑦ ᓱᕈᓰᑦ ᐊᐅᓪᓚᓚᐅᖅᓯᒪᙱᑉ<ᑕ, ᑎᑎᖅᑐᒐᖅᑎᓪᓗᒋᑦ ᐅᐸᓚᐅᖅᓯᒪᔪᒪᔭᒥᓄᑦ.

Where Have You Visited?

In this activity, children will share their personal experiences of or ideas about visiting a new place. Then they will draw a picture based on their experiences or ideas.

Directions

1. Ask the children if they remember where Solomon travelled to and why he went there. Ask them if they remember how Solomon felt while he was in Pond Inlet. You may choose to write down the children's answers.
2. Ask the children if they have ever travelled to a new place. If some or all of the children answer yes, prompt them to describe how they felt while they were in that new place. If some or all of the children answer no, ask them to think of a place they would like to visit and how they might feel if they were in that place. This place can be real or imagined.
3. To help the children think more about their experiences or ideas, you can ask them the following questions:
    - Why did you travel to this new place? Or why would you like to travel to this new place? For example, some people travel to go on vacation, to visit family, or for medical reasons.
    - How did you get to this place? Or how do people usually get to this place?
    - How did it feel to be away from home? Or how do you think it would feel?
    - How was this place similar to where you live, and how was it different? Or how do you think this place would be similar or different from where you live?
4. If some or all of the children have travelled to a new place, have them draw a picture of the place they have visited. If some or all of the children have never travelled to a new place, ask them to draw a picture of the place they would like to visit.

ᐃᓅᓯᓵᐅᑎᒃᑯᕕᒐ

ᐅᓇ ᐱᓕᕆᐊᒃᓴᖅ ᓱᕈᓯᕐᓄᑦ ᓇᓗᓇᐃᖅᓯᔾᔪᑕᐅᓂᐊᖅᑐᖅ ᐃᓅᓯᓵᐅᑎᒃᑯᕖᑦ ᑭᓱᑕᖃᓲᖑᒪᖔᑕ.

ᐊᔪᕆᖅᓯᐅᔾᔨᔾᔪᑎᑦ

1. ᒥᓇᕐᓗᒍ ᓴᖅᑭᓪᓗᒍᓗ ᐃᓅᓯᓵᐅᑎᒃᑯᕕᒐ ᐱᓕᕆᐊᒃᓴᖅ ᐅᕙᙵᑦ **www.arvaaq.com**.
2. ᐃᓕᓐᓂᐊᖅᑏᑦ ᐊᐱᕆᒃᑭᑦ ᖃᐅᔨᒪᖕᒪᖔᑕ ᐃᓅᓯᓵᐅᑎᒃᑯᕕᖕᒥ. ᖃᐅᔨᒪᙱᑉᐸᑕ, ᓇᓗᓇᐃᔭᐃᕕᒋᒃᑭᑦ ᐃᓅᓯᓵᐅᑎᒃᑯᕖᑦ ᐃᓗᓕᖃᐅᓲᖑᓂᖏᓐᓂᒃ ᐃᑲᔪᕈᑕᐅᓪᓗᑎᒃ ᖃᓂᒪᔪᓂᒃ ᐋᓐᓂᐊᔪᓂᓪᓘᓐᓃᑦ. ᐊᔪᕐᓇᙱᑉᐸᑦ, ᐃᓕᓐᓂᐊᖅᑏᑦ ᑕᑯᑎᒃᑭᑦ ᐃᓅᓯᓵᐅᑎᒃᑯᕕᖕᒥ ᐃᓗᓕᖕᒋᓐᓂᓪᓗ. ᐱᖁᓯᐅᔾᔭᔪᓐᓇᖅᑐᖅ ᒪᑦᑐᑎᒃᓴᓂᒃ, ᐳᔾᔫᖕᓂᒃ, ᐄᔭᒐᒃᑯᕕᖕᒥᒃ, ᐊᓪᓕᕉᔭᖕᓂᒃ, ᐆᓇᕐᓂᖅᓯᐅᒻᒥᒃ, ᐅᖅᓱᖅᑎᕈᒻᒥᒃ, ᐊᒃᑳᖕᓂᒃ, ᐊᒃᑲᓄᓪᓗ ᐃᕐᕉᒻᒥᒃ. ᓇᓗᓇᐃᔭᕐᓗᒋᑦ ᑭᓱᓄᑦ ᐊᑑᑎᖃᓲᖑᒪᖔᑕ.
3. ᐃᓕᓐᓂᐊᖅᑏᑦ ᐱᓕᕆᐊᒃᓴᒥᒃ ᑕᑯᑎᓪᓗᒋᑦ. ᓇᓗᓇᐃᖅᓯᕐᑯᓗᒋᑦ ᑭᓱᑦ ᐃᓅᓯᓵᐅᑎᒃᑯᕕᖕᒦᒃᑲᔭᕐᒪᖔᑕ. (ᐃᑲᔪᕆᐊᓖᑦ ᐃᑲᔪᕐᓗᒋᑦ.)
4. ᐃᓕᓐᓂᐊᖅᑏᑦ ᐊᒥᐊᕆᕐᑯᒃᑭᑦ ᐃᓅᓯᓵᐅᑎᒃᑯᕕᖕᒦᒃᑲᔭᖅᑐᒋᔭᖕᒋᓐᓂᒃ.
5. ᐃᓕᓐᓂᐊᖅᑏᑦ ᑕᑯᑎᓪᓗᒋᑦ ᐃᓅᓯᓵᐅᑎᒃᑯᕕᙳᐊᒥᒃ ᑐᓪᓕᐊᓂ ᐱᓕᕆᐊᒃᓴᒥ. ᐊᒥᐊᕆᕐᑯᒃᑭᑦ ᐃᓅᓯᓵᐅᑎᒃᑯᕕᙳᐊᒥᒃ.

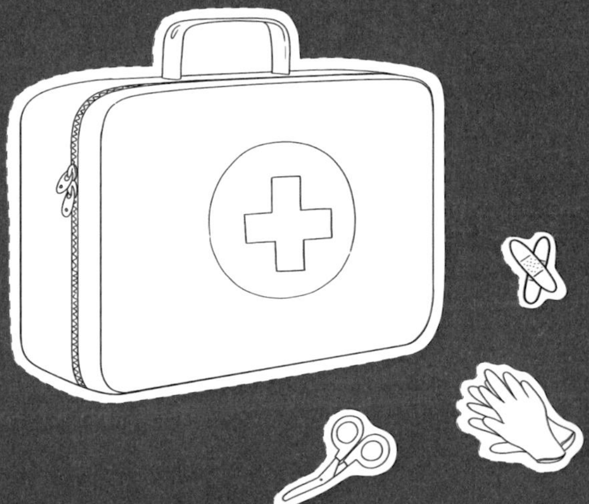

6. ᐃᓕᓐᓂᐊᖅᑎᑦ ᐅᑭᑎᕐᑯᒃᑭᑦ ᐃᓅᓯᓵᐅᑎᒃᑯᕕᙳᐊᒥᒃ ᐃᓗᓕᕆᒐᔭᙳᐊᖅᑕᖕᒋᓐᓂᓪᓗ. (ᐃᑲᔪᕆᐊᓖᑦ ᐃᑲᔪᕐᓗᒋᑦ.)
7. ᓂᐳᑎᕐᑲᖅᑎᓪᓗᑎᑦ ᐃᓕᓐᓂᐊᖅᑎᓪᓗ ᓂᐱᑎᑦᑎᕐᑲᑦᑕᕐᓗᑎᒃ ᐃᓅᓯᓵᐅᑎᙳᐊᓂᒃ ᐃᓅᓯᓵᐅᑎᒃᑯᕕᙳᐊᑉ ᑐᓄᐊᓄᑦ. (ᐃᑲᔪᕆᐊᓖᑦ ᐃᑲᔪᕐᓗᒋᑦ.)

My First Aid Kit

This activity will help children identify items that are found inside a first aid kit.

Directions

1. Download and print the My First Aid Kit worksheets from **www.arvaaq.com**.
2. Ask the children if they know what a first aid kit is. If they don't know what it is, explain that a first aid kit is a set of items that are used to help someone who is sick or hurt. If possible, show the children a first aid kit and some of the items inside it. This could include bandages, tweezers, a medicine bottle, scissors, a thermometer, a tube of ointment, gloves, and hand sanitizer. Describe what each item is used for.
3. Show the children the images on the first worksheet. Ask them to identify which items might be found inside a first aid kit and which items might not be found inside a first aid kit. (Assist as needed.)
4. Ask the children to colour the items that they think would be inside a first aid kit.
5. Show the children the image of the first aid kit on the second worksheet. Ask them to colour the first aid kit.
6. Have the children cut out the first aid kit and the items that they think would be inside it. (Assist as needed.)
7. Provide glue sticks and have the children glue the first aid kit items onto the back of the first aid kit. (Assist as needed.)

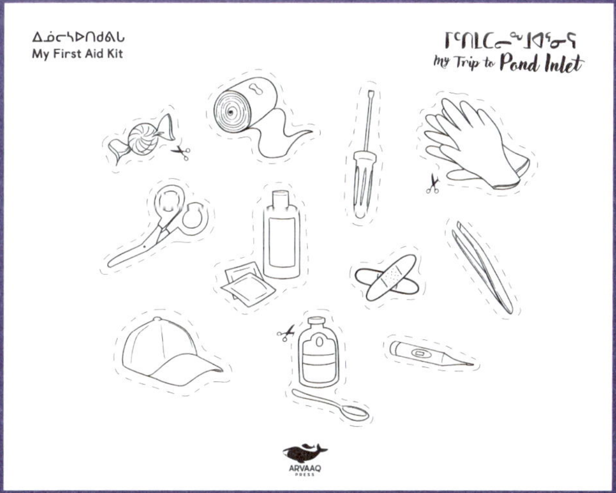

ARVAAQ
PRESS